D1631438

UNZIP YOUR LIPS

Paul Cookson was born in 1961 and brought up in Lancashire. His early ambitions were to play football for Everton or electric guitar in Slade but he eventually qualified and worked as a full time teacher for five years.

Since 1989 he has performed his poetry in thousands of venues all over the country. He is widely anthologized and has edited a number of poetry titles.

Paul often works with David Harmer in the popular performance poetry duo Spill the Beans and has appeared on radio and television, most recently on *Wham Bam Strawberry Jam!* for BBC Children's Television.

He lives in Retford, Nottinghamshire with his wife, Sally, and son, Sam.

UNZIP YOUR LIPS

Chosen by Paul Cookson

MACMILLAN
CHILDREN'S BOOKS

For Sally and Sam.

First published 1998
by Macmillan Children's Books
a division of Macmillan Publishers Ltd
25 Eccleston Place, London SW1W 9NF
and Basingstoke

Associated companies throughout the world

ISBN 0 333 73961 2

3 5 7 9 8 6 4

A CIP catalogue record for this book is available from the British Library.

Printed by Mackays of Chatham plc, Chatham, Kent.

Contents

Spell to Banish a Pimple

Get back pimple
get back to where you belong

Get back to never-never land
and I hope you stay there long

Get back pimple
get back to where you belong

How dare you take up residence
in the middle of my face

I never offered you a place
beside my dimple

Get back pimple
get back to where you belong

Get packing pimple
I banish you to outer space

If only life was that simple.

John Agard

A Smile

Smiling is infectious,
you catch it like the flu.
When someone smiled at me today
I started smiling too.

I passed around the corner
and someone saw my grin.
When he smiled, I realized
I'd passed it on to him.

I thought about my smile and then
I realized its worth.
A single smile like mine could travel
right around the earth.

If you feel a smile begin
don't leave it undetected.
Let's start an epidemic quick
and get the world infected.

Jez Alborough

Everybody Rap

Can you do a rap?
          Can you do a rap?
Can you make a rhyme?
          Can you make a rhyme?
Can you link up words,
          Can you link up words,
To help me blow my mind?
          To help me blow my mind?

     Poetry's the thing
     that we can do
     To show there's no difference
     Between me and you.

Black and white
are all the same
And those who say different
are mad insane.

     Do you agree?
     I said do you agree?
     If you agree,
     Say yowl to me.

SuAndi

My Gran

My Gran is
      a giggle-in-the-corner-like-a-child
            kind of Gran

She is
      a put-your-cold-hand-in-my-pocket
      a keep-your-baby-curls-in-my-locket
            kind of Gran

She is
      a make-it-better-with-a-treacle-toffee
      a what-you-need's-a-cup-of-milky-coffee
      a hurry-home-I-love-you-awfully
            kind of Gran

She is
      a butter-ball-for-your-bad-throat
      a stitch-your-doll-a-new-green-coat
      a let's-make-soapy-bubbles-float
      a hold-my-hand-I'm-seasick-in-a boat
            kind of Gran

She is
      a toast-your-tootsies-by-the-fire
      a crack-the-wishbone-for-your-heart's-desire
      a ladies-don't-sweat-they-perspire
      a funny-old-fashioned-higgledy-piggledy-lady-to-admire
            kind of Gran

And this lovely grandmother
          is mine, all mine!

Moira Andrew

Micky Hackett's Rocket

Micky Hackett
Built a rocket
From a bracket
And a sprocket.
"Look, Dicky! Book your ticket."
Dicky tried to nick it.
"I'll knock it, kick it, crack it."
They were making such a racket,
Dad took it, tried to pack it
In the pocket of his jacket.
But Mick – 'e's quick an' wicked –
Said "Dick, let's see you dock it.
Sneak it out and hook it
To the cooker.
Stick it
Crooked
In the socket
And tack it."
Wow! What a shock! It
Knocked Dad back. It
Crackled, smoked, and blackened
A mackerel, some cheese crackers,
Dad's mac, a tennis racquet,
And a packet of Mum's stockings.

Mum raised a raucous ruckus.
Smacked 'em, made 'em chuck it
All mucky in the bucket.
Dad whacked 'em,
Thwacked 'em,
Kicked 'em
Up to their room and locked it.

Leo Aylen

A Tale of Two Citizens

I have a Russian friend who lives in Minsk
And wears a lofty hat of beaver skinsk,
(Which does not suit a man so tall and thinsk).
He has a frizzly beard upon his chinsk.
He keeps his britches up with safety pinsk.
    "They're so much better than those thingsk
    Called belts and bracekies, don't you thinksk?"
    You'll hear him say, the man from Minsk.

He has a Polish pal who's from Gdansk,
Who lives by selling drinksk to football fansk,
And cheese rolls, from a little caravansk.
(He finds it pleasanter than robbing banksk.)
He also uses pinsk to hold his pantsk.
    "Keep up one's pantsk with rubber bandsk!?
    It can't be donesk! It simply can'tsk!
    Not in Gdansk!" he'll say. "No thanksk!"

They're so alikesk that strangers often thinksk
That they are brothers, yesk, or even twinsk.
"I live in Minsk but I was born in Omsk,"
Says one. His friend replies, "That's where *I'm* fromsk!
Perhapsk we're brothers after all, not friendsk."
    So they wrote homesk and asked their Mumsk
    But found they weren'tsk; so they shook handsk
    And left for Minsk, and for Gdansk.

Gerard Benson

Duppy Dance

You walk too-too late at night
duppies make your wrong road the right.
Around you, they rattle strings of bones.
    And duppies dance. Duppies dance.

All along deep-deep dark road
duppies croak like one hidden mighty toad.
You hear scary bells toll.
    And duppies dance. Duppies dance.

Duppies make horses-hooves clop-clop.
Make strange big birds flutter up.
Make you feel skin gone shrivelled.
    And duppies dance. Duppies dance.

Roaring ten bulls like one bull
duppies rip off your clothes in one pull.
Skeletons prance around you.
    And duppies dance. Duppies dance.

James Berry

Duppy = a Caribbean word meaning a ghost

Haircut Rap

Ah sey, ah want it short,
Short back an' side,
Ah tell him man, ah tell him
When ah teck him aside,
Ah sey, ah want a haircut
Ah can wear with pride,
So lef' it long on top
But short back an' side.

Ah sey try an' put a pattern
In the shorter part,
Yuh could put a skull an' crossbone,
Or an arrow through a heart,
Meck sure ah have enough hair lef'
Fe cover me wart,
Lef a likkle pon the top,
But the res' – keep it short.

Well, bwoy, him start to cut
An' me settle down to wait,
Him was cuttin' from seven
Till half-past eight,
Ah was startin' to get worried
'cause ah see it gettin' late,
But then him put the scissors down
Sey "There yuh are, mate."

Well ah did see a skull an a
Criss-cross bone or two,
But was me own skull an bone
That was peepin' through,
Ah look jus' like a monkey
Ah did see once at the zoo,
Him sey, "What's de matter, Tammy,
Don't yuh like the hair-do?"

Well, ah feel me heart stop beatin'
When me look pon me reflection,
Ah feel like somet'ing frizzle up
Right in me middle section
Ah look aroun' fe somewhey
Ah could crawl into an' hide
The day ah mek me brother cut
Me hair short back an' side.

Val Bloom

Tidyholic

My Mum's a tidyholic
Everything folded
Everything neat
All in its place
Never a heap
Never a pile
Never scattered
Always filed
Mum goes ballistic
She's never realistic
About the state of my room
I could fly to the moon
or meet my doom
As long as it's left spick and span
She'll love me then
Wherever I am.

Margaret Blount

The Shapeshifter's Riddle

I am the cat that leaps in my lap
I am the grey mouse caught in a trap
I am the yawn at the end of the day
I am the love that would love Spring to stay.

I am the hurt of the knee that is cut
I am the door that is open or shut
I am the longing to see the sun rise
I am the joy in the vast starry skies.

I am the oak branch   I am the bird
I am the paper   I am the word
I am the child   I am the man
I am the bridge   I am the span

I am older   Never old
I am bolder   Never bold
I am crying   Now I smile
I am an inch   I am a mile
I am a day   I am a night
I am the darkness   I am the light
I am a minute   I am a year
I am arriving   Not quite here
I am becoming   Always try
So pray then   Tell me
Who am   I?

Stephen Bowkett

Catnap in the Catnip
(after Kenneth Grahame)

Down among the catmint
By the garden wall,
Cats are a-sniffing,
Up tails all.

Black cats, white cats,
Ginger cats and tabby;
Fat cats, slight cats,
The skinny and the flabby.

Long cats, sleek cats,
Tortoiseshell and brindly;
Strong cats, weak cats,
The sturdy and the spindly.

House cats, mouse cats,
Pouncers and catchers;
Lost cats, cross cats,
The howlers and the scratchers.

Stray cats, fighting cats,
Every common moggy;
Day cats, night cats,
The fluffy and the soggy.

Street cats, fleet cats,
In and out the shadows;
Tree cats, free cats,
Hunting in the meadows.

Rich, bitch, kitsch cats,
Catty cats and spiteful;
Tough, gruff, rough cats,
Ratty cats and biteful.

Bold cats, young cats,
Stirrers and yowlers;
Old and highly-strung cats,
The purrers and the growlers.

Round cats, straight cats,
Every tiny kitten;
Grossly overweight cats,
The bruisers and flea-bitten.

They're sniffing at the catmint
By the garden wall;
Tranced cataleptic,
Up tails all.

Sandy Brownjohn

Assembly

I don't want to see any racing in the corridor,
a gentle glide's what we expect in here;
not that I mind a little heavy-handed fear
but you high spirits must slow down.

And I've had complaints that some of you
slip out at playtime. Let it be quite clear
that you stay in the graveyard till you hear
the bell. The chippy's out of bounds,
so is the sweetshop and your other favourite haunts.
I'll stop your little fun and groans:
there'll be a year's detention in the dungeons
for anyone caught chewing anything but bones.

And we'll have no more silly tricks with slamming doors,
at your age you should be walking through the walls.
And it isn't nice to use your loose heads as footballs
or vanish when you're being spoken to.

And finally, I really must remind you
that moans are not allowed before midnight,
especially near the staffroom. It's impolite
and disturbs the creatures – I mean teachers –
resting in despair and mournful gloom.
You there – stop wriggling in your coffin, I can't
bear to see a scruffy ghost –
put your face back where it was this instant
or you won't get to go howling at the moon.

Class Three, instead of double Shrieking
you'll do Terminal Disease with Dr Cyst;
Class Two stays here for Creepy Sneaking.
The rest of you can go. School dismissed.

Dave Calder

Out in the Desert

Out in the desert lies the sphinx
It never eats and it never drinx
Its body quite solid without any chinx
And when the sky's all purples and pinx
(As if it was painted with coloured inx)
And the sun it ever so swiftly sinx
Behind the hills in a couple of twinx
You may hear (if you're lucky) a bell that clinx
And also tolls and also tinx
And they say at the very same sound the sphinx
It sometimes smiles and it sometimes winx:

But nobody knows just what it thinx.

Charles Causley

My Sari

Saris hang on the washing line:
a rainbow in our neighbourhood.
This little orange one is mine,
it has a mango leaf design.
I wear it as a Rani would.
It wraps around me like sunshine,
it ripples silky down my spine,
and I stand tall and feel so good.

Debjani Chatterjee

Wrestling with Mum

Mum says, "Let's fight."
I say, "Not tonight."
But she nabs me, grabs me
twists and Boston Crabs me
lifts me
shifts me
Back Hammer
Body Slammer
Scissor Lock
Forearm Block
Arm Bender
Up Ender
Back Breaker
Widow Maker
Knee Drop
Karate Chop
Leg Split
SUBMIT
NO
Meat Cleaver
Arm Lever
Bear Hug
Finger Tug
Forearm Smash
Death Crash
Head Butt
Upper Cut
Shoulder Barge
Depth Charge
Arm Screw

follow through
Shoulder Press
No
Yes
No
Yes
1
2
3
PINFALL!
"Now tell me. What did you do at school?"

John Coldwell

What is an Alien?

He's the creak of your door
left open at night,
he's the whistle of wind
or a trick of the light.

He's the blink of a star
shooting through space,
he's the stranger next door,
he's a mystery face.

He's a tap on your window
when others don't hear,
he's the rattle of milk bottles,
when morning is near.

He's the tiny footsteps
left in the dew,
he's an alien creature
out of the blue.

Andrew Collett

Sea Shoals See Shows on the Sea Bed

The salmon with a hat on was conducting with a baton
and it tried to tune the tuna fish by playing on its scales
the scales had all been flattened when the tuna fish was sat on
on purpose by a porpoise and a school of killer whales.

So the salmon with a hat on fiddled with a baton
while the angel fish got ready to play the tambourine.
Things began to happen when the salmon with a baton
was tapping out a pattern for the band of the marines.

There was a minnow on piano, a prawn with a horn,
an otter on guitar looking all forlorn.
A whale voice choir and a carp with a harp,
a belly dancing jelly fish jiving with a shark.

The octaves on the octopus played the middle eight
but they couldn't keep in time with the skiffle playing skate.
The plaice on the bass began to rock and roll
with the bloater in a boater and a Dover sole.

A clam on castanets, an eel on glockenspiel,
an oyster in a cloister singing with a seal.
The haddock had a headache from the deafening din
and the sword dancing sword fish sliced off a fin.

A limpet on a trumpet, a flat fish on a flute,
the kipper fell asleep with King Canute.
Barracuda on a tuba sat upon a rock,
the electric eel gave everyone a shock.

The shrimp and the sturgeon, the stingray and the squid
sang a four part harmony on the sea bed.
The crab and the lobster gave their claws a flick,
kept everyone in time with their click click click...
kept everyone in time with their click click click...
kept everyone in time with their click click click.

Yes the salmon with a hat on was tapping out a pattern
and things began to happen for the band of the marines.
It was an ocean of commotion of Atlantic proportion
the greatest show by schools of shoals
that ever had been seen.

Paul Cookson

Haiku

To convey one's mood
in seventeen syllables
is very diffic

John Cooper-Clarke

An Attempt at Unrhymed Verse

People tell you all the time,
Poems do not have to rhyme.
It's often better if they don't
And I'm determined this one won't.
               Oh dear.

Never mind, I'll start again.
Busy, busy with my pen . . . cil.
I can do it if I try –
Easy, peasy, pudding and gherkins.

Writing verse is so much fun,
Cheering as the summer weather,
Makes you feel alert and bright,
'Specially when you get it more or less the way
                       you want it.

Wendy Cope

The Playground Monster

It grabbed me
with its tarmac jaws
and then it tried
to bite me.

It grasped me
with its gravelly paws
and then it tried
to fight me.

I live in fear of walking
across its great black back.

I think it knows I'm talking.
It listens at a crack!

I fear its greedy darkness,
the way it seems to need

to reach out when I'm running
and grab me for a feed.

It grabbed me
with its tarmac jaws
and then it tried
to bite me.

It grasped me
with its gravelly paws
and then it tried
to fight me.

Pie Corbett

Class Three's Affections

Jim is most fond of Mary
And Mary's attracted to Joe,
While Joe thinks a lot of Rebecca
Who sits in the class's front row.

But Rebecca has quiet thoughts about Basil,
As Basil dreams of sweet Beth,
And Beth each time she sees Ali
She finds herself quite out of breath.

Ali sends small notes to Kirsty
That hint at how much he cares,
Although Kirsty is taken with Eric
And the lovely green jacket he wears.

While Eric thinks Sita is charming,
I fear Sita thinks coolly of him.
She'd rather be liked by his classmate
The lively and oh so smart Jim.

But Jim is most fond of Mary
Which is where we began as you know,
So when it comes to affection and liking
The classroom is warm and aglow.

Yet shyness prevents them all saying,
So their secret affections aren't shared,
Except for one heart and initials
In the bike shed where somebody dared.

John Cotton

Well, You Shouldn't Have ...

Er, Mum – I've just had an explosion.
Well, you shouldn't have shaken your drink!

Er, Mum, – I've just flooded the bathroom.
Well, you shouldn't have blocked up the sink!

Er, Mum – I've just spilt Grandad's maggots.
Well, you shouldn't have been in the shed!

Er, Mum – I've just tidied my bedroom.
Well, you shouldn't have ... WHAT'S that you said?

Sue Cowling

Standing Up to Read a Poem in Front of All These People

I've got to do it,
Sir says so,
And we've been practising
For weeks.
We missed games last night,
To have a
Final Rehearsal.
I've got to do it,
Because Sir's picked me,
And Mam says she'll be proud,
But Sir says NOT TOO LOUD
And don't rush it;
But I feel sure
I'll mess it up.
It'll be all right
If I remember how it should go,
And our Jim doesn't pick his nose,
In the front row,
And make me laugh.
So here goes . . .
. . . .
Damn . . .
How does it begin?

John Cunliffe

Ghosts In Our Suburban Homes

The creaking of a wicker chair
When something unseen settles there.
It's ghosts, ss, ss, ss . . . It's ghosts.

Mad wardrobes swinging in the night,
A flicker at the edge of sight –
It's ghosts, ss, ss, ss . . . It's ghosts.

The rocker rocks. The curtains sigh,
Out of the corner of your eye
The solid darkness passes by – it's ghosts!

They spread themselves along the wall –
Shadows with shadows haunt the hall,
A great grey silent waterfall . . . of ghosts!

Come midnight, watch the stair-
Tread sink with no foot there.
It's ghosts, ss, ss, ss . . . It's ghosts.

A thousand thousand whispering souls
Mass quietly behind small holes.
A million slither through the cracks
Behind the door, behind our backs
Insinuating, white as wax . . . are ghosts!

And in the silence of the moon,
The silver silence of the moon,
The ghosts release a silent tune
To rise like steam from some sad tomb.
The soundless song of frozen skies,
The ice of unsung lullabies,
Wordless as the frosted eyes of ghosts . . .

Ghosts in our suburban homes.
Ghosts in our suburban homes.
Ghosts, ss, ss, ss,
Ghosts.

Jan Dean

Team Talk

We're up against a team
that knows its onions –
not much about football.
It's the way they play
that makes you cry.

Including the sub.
It's the "dirty dozen";
the shin hackers, shirt pullers
and elbow diggers.

We are going to show them,
expose them for what they are,
embarrass them from the kick off,
unnerve them with new tactics
of very close marking.

As soon as the whistle blows
you turn to the nearest man
and pull his shorts down.

John C. Desmond

Meryl Rose

Here's a tale of Meryl Rose
Who liked to push things up her nose . . .
    Lego biscuits
             Beads and bread –
                    Rattled round inside her head.

A foolish girl – who wasted days
Playing with her silly craze –

Until upon school photo day
She got the hamster out to play,
And with a grin and Meryl pout
She pushed poor Hammy up her snout!

"Look this way," called photo man
"Smile or giggle if you can . . ."

    Sweet Meryl posed
           with smile
               and pout –

And half a hamster hanging out!

                      Peter Dixon

Night Mer

One night when I was fast appeels
all duggled snown and warm
I had a very dasty ream
about a stunder thorm
and fightning lashed
and saves at wea
like boiling werpents sithed
and foaming angs did frockle me
and shicked and slucked and eyethed.
They ulled me under, lungings full
of fevvered, fluffin fug
till suffing grably I apized
upon the redroom bug.

Gina Douthwaite

Chocs

Into the half-pound box of Moonlight
my small hand crept.
There was an electrifying rustle.
There was a dark and glamorous scent.
Into my open, moist mouth
the first Montelimar went.

Down in the crinkly second layer,
five finger-piglets snuffled
among the Hazelnut Whirl,
the Caramel Square,
the Black Cherry and Almond Truffle.

Bliss.

I chomped. I gorged.
I stuffed my face,
till only the Coffee Cream
was left for the owner of the box –
tough luck, Anne Pope –
oh, and half an Orange Supreme.

                    Carol Ann Duffy

Some Favourite Words

Mugwump, chubby, dunk and whoa,
Swizzle, doom and snoop,
Flummox, lilt and afterglow,
Gruff, bamboozle, whoop
And nincompoop.

Wallow, jungle, lumber, sigh,
Ooze and zodiac,
Innuendo, lullaby,
Ramp and mope and quack
And paddywhack.

Moony, undone, lush and bole,
Inkling, tusk, guffaw,
Waspish, croon and cubby-hole,
Fern, fawn, dumbledore
And many more . . .

Worm.

Richard Edwards

Shaun Short's Short Shorts

Shaun Short bought some shorts.
The shorts were shorter than Shaun Short thought.
Shaun Short's short shorts were so short,
Shaun Short thought, *Shaun, you ought*
Not to have bought shorts so short.

John Foster

A Perfect Match

We met in Nottingham Forest,
    My sweet Airdrie and I.
She smiled and said, "Alloa!" to me –
    Oh, never say goodbye!

I asked her, "Is your Motherwell?"
    And she replied, "I fear
She's got the Academicals
    From drinking too much beer."

We sat down on a Meadowbank
    And of my love I spoke.
"Queen of the South," I said to her,
    "My fires of love you Stoke."

We went to Sheffield, Wednesday.
        Our Hearts were one. Said she,
"Let's wed in Accrington, Stanley,
        Then we'll United be."

The ring was Stirling silver.
        Our friends, Forfar and wide,
A motley Crewe, all gathered there
        And fought to kiss the bride.

The best man had an awful lisp.
        "Come Raith your glatheth up,"
He said, and each man raised on high
        His Coca-Cola Cup.

The honeymoon was spent abroad:
        We flew out east by Ayr,
And found the far-off Orient
        Partick-ularly fair.

We're home, in our own Villa now,
        (The Walsall painted grey)
And on our Chesterfield we sit
        And watch Match of the Day.

Pam Gidney

Wurd Up

Blowin like a hurricane
Destroyin all the competishan
Kickin up the lirix hard
There ain't no opposishan
Coz
Wen I'm on a roll like this
I'm jus like a physishan
Like a boxer . . . punch you out
With lirical precishan
Flowin like a river
Jus
Flyin like a bird
'N'
Checkin out the ridim
Jus takin in my wurdz
It'z time
Ter climb
'n' rime
The sign
Jus growz
'n' flowz
'n' showz
'n' throwz
a skill
Ter thrill
'n' kill
Jus chill
Coz
I'm
Stingin like a nettle

Jus bitin like a flea
Smoother than a baby's skin
Much ruffer than the sea
Colder than an icicle
Hotta than the sun
Lirix always on the move
Like bullets from a gun
Much noizier than thunder
Much cooler than the rain
I'm fitta than an exercise
Deep within the brain
Sharpa than a needle
More solid than a rock
Repeatin like an echo
As rhythmic as a clock
More dangerus than a lion
Much louda than a plane
As quiet as a whisper
I burn yer like a flame
Fasta than a jaguar
Slowa than a snail
Yeah! rapid like a heartbeat
Tuffa than a nail
More painful than a scratch
As tasty as food
Horrible like a medicine
My lirix change yer mood
As tasty as a mango
As bitter as a lime
Softa than a coconut
Endless as the time

Kickin like a reggae song
Much sadda than the blues
I'm as tirin as a marathon
Give yer all the newz
Wilda than a stampede
As gentle as a breeze
Irritatin as a cough
More wicked than a sneeze
More lively than a child
Romantic that's me
Still harsh like the winter
Jus buzzin like a bee
The rimes 'n' times are signs
to blow 'n' show a flow

The wurdz

WURD UP!

Martin Glynn

Boots

It's chilly on the touch line, but
with all my kit on
underneath my clothes
I'm not too cold. Besides,
I've got a job to do:
     I'm Third Reserve
     I run the line.

I've been the Third Reserve all season,
every Saturday.
I've never missed a match.
At Home, Away:
It's all the same to me:
     'Cos I'm the third Reserve,
     The bloke who runs the line.

That's my reward
for turning up
to every practice session, every
circuit training. Everything.
No one else does that –
     To be the Third Reserve,
     To run the line.

No chance of substitutions.
Broken ankles on the pitch
mean someone else's chance, not mine.
One down –
       and still two more to go:
     When you're the Third Reserve
     You run the line.

When I was first made Third Reserve
my dad and me went out
and bought new boots. I keep them in the box.
I grease them every week and put them back.
        When you're the Third Reserve –
        you know the score –
You run the line in worn out-daps.

Mick Gowar

Daughter of the Sea

bog seeper
moss creeper
growing restless getting steeper

trickle husher
swish and rusher
stone leaper splash and gusher

foam flicker
mirror slicker
pebble pusher boulder kicker

still pool
don't be fooled
shadow tricker keeping cool

leap lunger
crash plunger
free fall with thunder under

garbage binner
dump it in her
never mind her dog's dinner

plastic bagger
old lagger
oil skinner wharf nagger

cargo porter
weary water
tide dragger long lost daughter

of the sea
the sea the sea
has caught her up in its arms and set her free

Philip Gross

41

Semantricks...

Ay phuri lid el kator pilla
Sed "Omi omi!
Owkana nugli slugli
Kiyam
Beer, butt or flie?
Snotwot yer dekspektatol,
Spastmi owit wurkz,
Dyerfink itzmeta
Morphiziz?
Dyerphinkidiz?
Off corsetiz!
Eye moffgot Wingsbye buy!"

Mike Harding

Mister Moore

Mister Moore, Mister Moore
Creaking down the corridor.

Uh uh eh eh uh
Uh uh eh eh uh

Mister Moore wears wooden suits
Mister Moore's got great big boots
Mister Moore's got hair like a brush
And Mister Moore don't like me much.

Mister Moore, Mister Moore
Creaking down the corridor.

Uh uh eh eh uh
Uh uh eh eh uh

When my teacher's there I haven't got a care
I can do my sums, I can do gerzinters
When Mister Moore comes through the door
Got a wooden head filled with splinters.

Mister Moore, Mister Moore
Creaking down the corridor.

Uh uh eh eh uh
Uh uh eh eh uh

Mister Moore I implore
My earholes ache, my head is sore
Don't come through that classroom door.
Don't come through that classroom door.

Mister Mister Mister Moore
He's creaking down the corridor.

Uh uh eh eh uh
Uh uh eh eh uh

Big voice big hands
Big feet he's a very big man
Take my advice, be good be very very nice
Be good be very very nice
To Mister Moore, Mister Moore
Creaking down the corridor.

Uh uh eh eh uh
Uh uh eh eh uh

Mister Moore wears wooden suits
Mister Moore's got great big boots
Mister Moore's got hair like a brush
Mister Moore don't like me much.

Mister Moore, Mister Moore
Creaking down the corridor.

Uh uh eh eh uh
Uh uh eh eh uh

David Harmer

The Painting Lesson

"What's THAT, dear?"
Asked the new teacher.

"It's Mummy,"
I replied.
"But mums aren't green and orange!
You really haven't TRIED.
You don't just paint in SPLODGES;
You're old enough to know
You need to THINK before you work.
Now – have another go."

She helped me draw two arms and legs,
A face with sickly smile,
A rounded body, dark brown hair,
A hat – and in a while
She stood back, with her face bright pink:
"That's SO much better, don't you think?"

But she turned white
At ten to three
When an orange-green blob
Collected me.

"Hi, Mum!"

Trevor Harvey

On the Pavement

Sauntering along alone I hear other busier footsteps
    behind me.
Not feeling threatened but awkward
I wonder, should I slow down my walking
and let them get by as soon as possible
or shall I imperceptibly quicken to a higher gear
before they are near enough to notice?
Ah, it's OK, it sounds like they've just fallen over.

John Hegley

Tiger

Through the grass the tiger stalks
another of his evening walks.
You never hear his silent stroll
as he pads near the water-hole.
It's not a place to stand and mope,
I'm glad I'm not an antelope.

Stewart Henderson

Best Friends

It's Susan I talk to not Tracey,
Before that I sat next to Jane;
I used to be best friends with Lynda
But these days I think she's a pain.

Natasha's all right in small doses,
I meet Mandy sometimes in town;
I'm jealous of Annabel's pony
And I don't like Nicola's frown.

I used to go skating with Catherine,
Before that I went there with Ruth;
And Kate's so much better at trampoline:
She's a show-off, to tell you the truth.

I think that I'm going off Susan,
She borrowed my comb yesterday;
I think I might sit next to Tracey,
She's my nearly best friend: she's OK.

Adrian Henri

Just Fancy That ...

I really fancy Phillip Strong
But Phillip's just nuts about Dee.
Danya's mad over Andrew Moore . . .
And John –
He loves MUFC.

I'm really smitten with Steven Myers
But Steven's fallen for Toni.
Freddy thinks Thea's fantastically fit . . .
And Pauline –
Her pash is her pony.

I've got a real crush on Corin Walsh
But Corin's sweet on Sujatha.
Sudeep's all sloppy over John's sister, Poppy . . .
and Adam –
Just adores his computer.

I've got a real thing for that cute Ian King –
I just know I'll get left on the shelf.
Sasha's gone spoony over Sam who's just moved here . . .
And Claire –
She's in love with herself.

I'm ever so keen on Kevin MacLean
But I've heard Dee's packed in Phillip Strong.
And anyway Kevin's into cross country running . . .
And I –
Really fancied Phillip all along.

David Horner

Shop Chat

My shop stocks:
>   locks, chips,
>   chopsticks,
>   watch straps,
>   traps, tops,
>   taps, tricks,
>   ship's clocks,
>   lipstick and chimney pots.

What does your shop stock?

>   *Sharkskin socks.*

Libby Houston

My Granny

My Granny is an octopus
    At the bottom of the sea,
And when she comes to supper
    She brings her family.

She chooses a wild wet windy night
    When the world rolls blind
As a boulder in the night-sea surf,
    And her family troops behind.

The sea-smell enters with them
    As they sidle and slither and spill
With their huge eyes and their tiny eyes
    And a dripping ocean-chill.

Some of her cousins are lobsters
    Some floppy jellyfish –
What would you be if your family tree
    Grew out of such a dish?

Her brothers are crabs jointed and knobbed
    With little pinhead eyes,
Their pincers crack the biscuits
    And they bubble joyful cries.

Crayfish the size of ponies
    Creak as they sip their milk.
My father stares in horror
    At my mother's secret ilk.

They wave long whiplash antennae,
    They sizzle and they squirt –
We smile and waggle our fingers back
    Or Grandma would be hurt.

"What's new, Ma?" my father asks,
    "Down in the marvellous deep?"
Her face swells up, her eyes bulge huge
    And she begins to weep.

She knots her sucker tentacles
    And gapes like a nestling bird,
And her eyes flash, changing stations,
    As she attempts a WORD –

Then out of her eyes there brim two drops
    That plop into her saucer –
And that is all she manages,
    And my Dad knows he can't force her.

And when they've gone, my ocean-folk
    No man could prove they came –
For the sea-tears in her saucer
    And a man's tears are the same.

Ted Hughes

My Shops

I love a shop that almost sings
With bright, unnecessary things,

Little ornaments and toys,
All that one like me enjoys,

I never want to see a shop
That sells a carrot or pork chop,

But when a music-box I see,
I know the shop was meant for me.

Shops with windows full of hats
Are boring. I want china cats.

Supermarkets make me feel
I never want another meal.

But knicks and knacks of every kind
Were made for me and store my mind.

Hurroo Hurrah, Hurroo Hurray!
Today's my kind of shopping day!

                    Elizabeth Jennings

Iced Ink
The Punk Skunk's Song

Sing a punk skunk's song:
if you like to pong;
if you like to whiff;
if you like to stink,
after me, shout out "Iced ink!"

Try it twice a week,
if you like to reek
like a goat or polecat,
maybe a mink;
after me, shout "Iced ink!"

If there's dust or dirt
clinging to your shirt,
if your underwear
should be in the sink,
after me, shout out "Iced ink!"

If you never clench
your nose at the stench,
when your nostril shocks
make the vicar blink,
after me, shout out "Iced ink!"

If foul odour wafts
from your unwashed socks;
if your noxious feet
tend to tarnish zinc,
after me, shout out "Iced ink!"

Sing a punk skunk's song:
if you like to pong;
if you like to whiff;
if you like to stink,
after me, shout out "Iced ink!"

Mike Johnson

Going Out With Mum

"Still got the umbrella Dad gave me last Christmas.
Just fetch my gloves dear, no, the leather ones,
The ones I went to Baker Street to collect
And the man said 'All change' and wouldn't let me stop
To think if I had everything.
Look in the other drawer. Have you seen my purse, John?
I know I had it, I'd just paid the milkman
And the phone rang. Look in the bathroom then.
Keys, money, letters. Have you got handkerchiefs?
Don't sniff, Bridget, blow. I must make sure
I've got the address right. D'you think you'd better take
  macs?
Just put the bread knife away dear, you never know
Who may get in and if they see one handy
It might – no, leave the kitchen window
There's the cat."

We round the corner as the bus pulls off
From the bus stop. "Now if you'd been ready
We might have caught that. It would have made all the
  difference.
There might not be another one for hours."

We almost believe it's true it was our fault:
Mum's too good at being efficient for it to be hers.

Jenny Joseph

55

Rockets

Rockets are the only *real* fireworks!

You can keep your Catherine wheels that stick.
You can stick your rotten Roman candles and
your feeble fountains that hiss and splutter,
pretty-pretty-tinkle-silver snow-storms that
                                    drop down dead.

Give me rockets instead!

Rockets get off to a flying start.
They dart and dash,
    they flash
        crash
        smash
    and splash their exploding cascades of colour
on the blue-black sky.
Hurtling high,
rockets fly furiously.
They zip,
    and rip in the night, excitedly,
in a swooshing frantic flight, ready to burst, until,
            at their height,
the first thunderous crack attacks your ears, and
a galaxy of shooting stars spreads in all directions.

Rockets whistle and scream
                and send teeming, snap-crackling sparkling
                        star-streams
of cosmic red, green nebula and galactic gold.

On a cold, bright November night,
    you can keep your fountains that fizz. Half-hearted fireworks.

Give me the daring, sky-tearing whoosh and whizz of

R			
O			R
C	R	R	O
K	O	O	C
E	C	C	K
T	K	K	E
S	E	E	T
	T	T	S
	S	S	

Mike Jubb

Hairpin Bend

Around the hairpin
bends
    where the drop
down
    gives you vertigo
and
    you cling
to the steering wheel,
    there are
    mountain goats
who
    ring their bells
while
    you get dizzy
        and even
        dizzier,
they are just happy –
long beards
        shaking –
probably
    laughing
        a goat's guffaw
at the tourist's
        silly fear of heights.

Aaaargh. Help.

Jackie Kay

58

The Newcomer

Don't make a whisper –
    don't make a sound –
poor old Last Year's
    gone to ground.
Snoozing and snorting,
    he won't come back
though the icicles crinkle
    and the high wires crack.

Listen a moment . . .
    can you hear
something delicate
    drawing near,
little and faint
    and far away?
Those are the steps
    of New Year's Day.

New Year's bright with gold.
    He wears
bells on his ankles,
    rings on his ears –
whistles and dances
    and taps his drum.
Run and put the kettle on –
    NEW YEAR's
        COME!

Jean Kenward

Nothing Tastes Quite Like a Gerbil

Nothing tastes quite like a gerbil
They're small and tasty to eat –
Morsels of sweet rodent protein
From whiskers to cute little feet!

You can bake them, roast them or fry them,
They grill nicely and you can have them *en croûte*,
In garlic butter they're simply delicious
You can even serve them with fruit.

So you can keep your beef and your chicken,
Your lamb and your ham on the bone,
I'll have gerbil as my daily diet
And what's more – I can breed them at home!

Tony Langham

2 Poems About 4 Eyes

They call me Specky Four Eyes.
I wear glasses, so it's true,
I can see quite well why you're teasing me,
I've got two more eyes than you.

My spectacles are magical
for when you taunt and jeer,
I only have to take them off
to make you disappear.

Lindsay MacRae

In the Misty, Murky Graveyard

In the misty, murky graveyard
    there's a midnight dance,
and in moonlight shaking skeletons
are twirling in a trance.
Linked arm in bony arm
they point and pitch and prance,
down there in the graveyard
    at the midnight dance.

In the misty, murky graveyard
    there's a midnight rave,
and a score of swaying skeletons
are lurching round a grave.
Their toe bones tip and tap
and their rattling fingers wave,
down there in the graveyard
    at the midnight rave.

In the misty, murky graveyard
    there's a midnight romp,
and the squad of skinless skeletons
all quiver as they stomp.
To the whistle of the wind
they clink and clank and clomp,
down there in the graveyard
    at the midnight romp.

Wes Magee

The Crunch

The lion and his tamer
They had a little tiff,
For the lion limped too lamely, –
The bars had bored him stiff.

No *call to crack your whip, Sir!*
Said the lion then irate:
No *need to snap my head off,*
Said the tamer – but too late.

Gerda Mayer

A Gottle of Geer
(to be read aloud without moving the lips)

I an a little wooden dunny
With a hand inside ny gack
How I niss ny daddy and nunny
Now the future's looking glack

Locked all day in a suitcase
I seldon see the sun
I've never tasted lenonade
Or a guttered hot cross gun

The owner takes ne out at night
To sit on his gony knee
He talks a load of ruggish
I think you will agree

Gut the audience go gananas
"Gravo!" "Gravo!" they cheer
As he drinks a glass of water
And I say: "A bottle of beer."

Roger McGough

Biggles Flies To Barnsley

Biggles Ginger Algy Bertie
They fought clean and never dirty
Biggles Bertie Algy Ginger
Smell of courage tends to linger
Biggles Ginger Bertie Algy
Jaws so manly chests so bulgy
Ginger Bertie Algy Biggles
No one laughs and no one giggles.

Biggles Ginger Algy Bertie
Always just this side of thirty
Biggles Algy Bertie Ginger
Eyes that blaze with righteous anger
Biggles Ginger Bertie Algy
Golden age of pure nostalgia
Ginger Bertie Algy Biggles
Pull those flipping parachute toggles.

Biggles Algy Ginger Bertie
Patriotic and alertie
Biggles Bertie Algy Ginger
Better than the turtles ninja
Biggles Ginger Bertie Algy
Old enough to get neuralgia
Ginger Bertie Algy Biggles
Looks like Douglas Hurd in goggles.

Ian McMillan and Martyn Wiley

Teef! Teef!

Teef! Teef!
I've loshed my teef!
Hash anyone sheen my teef?
You won't be able to help, I shuppose;
But shombody shtole them from
Under my nose!
Hash anyone sheen my teef?

Colin McNaughton

The Dark Avenger
for 2 voices

My dog is called The Dark Avenger.
Hello, I'm Cuddles.

She understands every word I say.
Woof?

Last night I took her for a walk.
Woof! Walkies! Let's go!

Cleverly, she kept 3 paces ahead.
I dragged him along behind me.

She paused at every danger, spying out the land.
I stopped at every lamp-post.

When the coast was clear, she sped on.
I slipped my lead and ran away.

Scenting danger, Avenger investigated.
I found some fresh chip papers in the bushes.

I followed, every sense alert.
He blundered through the trees, shouting "Oy, Come 'ere!
    Where are you?"

Something – maybe a sixth sense – told me to stop.
He tripped over me in the dark.

There was a pale menacing figure ahead of us.
Then I saw the white Scottie from next door.

Avenger sprang into battle, eager to defend his master.
Never could stand terriers!

They fought like tigers.
We scrapped like dogs.

Until the enemy was defeated.
Till Scottie's owner pulled him off – spoilsport!

Avenger gave a victory salute.
I rolled in the puddles.

And came to check I was all right.
I shook mud over him.

"Stop it, you stupid dog!"
He congratulated me.

Sometimes, even The Dark Avenger can go too far.
Woof!!

Trevor Millum

Dumb Insolence

I'm big for ten years old
Maybe that's why they get at me

Teachers, parents, cops
Always getting at me

When they get at me

I don't hit 'em
They can do you for that

I don't swear at 'em
They can do you for that

I stick my hands in my pockets
And stare at them

And while I stare at them
I think about sick

They call it dumb insolence

They don't like it
But they can't do you for it

Adrian Mitchell

Forbidden Poem

This poem is not for children.
Keep out!
There is a big oak door
in front of this poem.
It's locked.
And on the door is a notice
in big red letters.
It says: Any child who enters here
will never be the same again.
WARNING. KEEP OUT.

But what's this?
A key in the keyhole.
And what's more,
nobody's about.

"Go on. Look,"
says a little voice
inside your head.
"Surely a poem
cannot strike you dead?"

You turn the key.
The door swings wide.
And then you witness
what's inside.

And from that day
you'll try in vain.
You'll never be the same again.

Tony Mitton

Food for Thought

Slugs that slither near your mushrooms
Have a tendency to hide.
Look out when you take a mouthful,
Those chewier bits are soft inside.

Flies that settle on your biscuit
Stay so still and blend right in.
Look out for the bits that tickle
Just as you are swallowing.

Worms that wander near spaghetti
Lose their footing and fall in.
Look out, for that bit you're sucking
Look as as if it's wriggling.

If you sneeze when near green chutney
Have the goodness to confess,
Suspicious lumps and slimy green bits
Could occasion some distress.

If you're offered Irish stew
With meat and veg chunks brown and thick,
It might be kinder not to mention
That the dog has just been sick.

Michaela Morgan

Peasy!

You want me to do that ten figure sum,
    that's peasy!
Wind my legs over that bar,
slide down into a forward roll
with a double back flip to follow,
    that's peasy!
Build a working model of Big Ben
from Technical Lego,
    huh, peasy!
Clear that five foot hurdle in one leap,
cross country run up a mountain peak,
keep writing a story for one whole week,
    peeeeeeeeeasy!
Score thirty goals in record time,
in ten minutes write a thousand lines
say *Supercalifragilisticexpialidocious* two hundred times,
    backwards.
    Oh, that's far too peasy!
BUT . . .
Eat the skin off of custard.
Ugh! That's the toughest thing in the world.

                        Brian Moses

Caliban's Cave

The sand is damp
and cold as stone
when the tide creeps back
from Caliban's Cave.

The rocks are black
as you creep alone
on the dark, damp sand
of Caliban's Cave.

The seagulls sing
and the sea-shells moan
as they slide in the tide
through Caliban's Cave.

The pebbles ring
like the crack of a bone
as you tiptoe deep
into Caliban's Cave.

The music dies
when the waves have gone
and you stand alone
in Caliban's Cave . . .

You stand in the heart
of Caliban's Cave . . .

Judith Nicholls

Roller-Skaters

Flying by
on the winged-wheels
of their heels

Two teenage earthbirds
zig-zagging
down the street

Rising
unfeathered –
in sudden air-leap

Defying law
death and gravity
as they do a wheely

Landing back
in the smooth swoop
of youth

And faces gaping
gawking, impressed
and unimpressed

Only Mother watches – heartbeat in her mouth

Grace Nichols

Love Conquers All
(a love poem for dyslexics)

B you're adorable
M you're so beautiful
H you're as cute as can be
I may be dyslexic
but I'll try to spell it out
I lob yup

Henry Normal

Bigfoot

When you're sitting in a diner
In New York or Carolina
Just check on the person
In the next door seat:
If he's got a tie and collar on
You'd bet your bottom dollar on
Him being just the nicest guy
You'd ever want to meet,
BUT . . .
If his shoes are of colossal size
It won't take long to realize
The one thing he cannot disguise
is GREAT BIG FEET!
He hides his hair beneath his clothes
And hat – he's got a mask that goes
A long way to hiding his rather ugly face;
He speaks in clear American
He acts the perfect gentleman
You'd think he was a credit to the human race;
But you'd better be much warier
He's quite a good deal hairier
And considerably scarier
When lurking in the street,
So if you pass the time of day
There's one thing that you mustn't say
 – He really hates your mentioning
His GREAT BIG FEET!

David Orme

Gran Can You Rap?

Gran was in her chair she was taking a nap
When I tapped her on the shoulder to see if she could rap.
Gran can you rap? Can you rap? Can you Gran?
And she opened one eye and she said to me, Man,
  I'm the best rapping Gran this world's ever seen
  I'm a tip-top, slip-slap, rap-rap queen.

And she rose from her chair in the corner of the room
And she started to rap with a bim-bam-boom,
And she rolled up her eyes and she rolled round her head
And as she rolled by this is what she said,
  I'm the best rapping Gran this world's ever seen
  I'm a nip-nap, yip-yap, rap-rap queen.

Then she rapped past my dad and she rapped past my
    mother,
She rapped past me and my little baby brother.
She rapped her arms narrow she rapped her arms wide,
She rapped through the door and she rapped outside.
  She's the best rapping Gran this world's ever seen
  She's a drip-drop, trip-trap, rap-rap queen.

She rapped down the garden she rapped down the street,
The neighbours all cheered and they tapped their feet.
She rapped through the traffic lights as they turned red
As she rapped round the corner this is what she said,
  I'm the best rapping Gran this world's ever seen
  I'm a flip-flop, hip-hop, rap-rap queen.

She rapped down the lane she rapped up the hill,
And as she disappeared she was rapping still.
I could hear Gran's voice saying, Listen Man,
Listen to the rapping of the rap-rap Gran.
    I'm the best rapping Gran this world's ever seen
    I'm a –
        tip-top, slip-slap,
            nip-nap, yip-yap,
                hip-hop, trip-trap,
                    touch yer cap,
                    take a nap,
                        happy, happy, happy, happy,
                        rap____ rap ____ queen.

Jack Ousbey

The Commentator

Good afternoon and welcome
To this international
Between England and Holland
Which is being played here today
At 4, Florence Terrace.
And the pitch looks in superb condition
A Danny Markey, the England captain,
Puts England on the attack.
Straight away it's Markey
With a lovely little pass to Keegan,
Keegan back to Markey,
Markey in possession here
Jinking skilfully past the dustbins;
And a neat flick inside the cat there
What a brilliant player this Markey is
And he's still only nine years old!
Markey to Francis,
Francis back to Markey,
Markey is through, he's through,
No, he's been tackled by the drainpipe:
But he's won the ball back brilliantly
And he's advancing on the Dutch keeper,
It must be a goal.
The keeper's off his line
But Markey chips him superbly
And it's a goal
No!
It's gone into Mrs Spence's next door.
And Markey's going round to ask for his ball back,
It could be the end of this international.
Now the door's opening

And yes, it's Mrs Spence,
Mrs Spence has come to the door
Wait a minute
She's shaking her head, she's shaking her head
She's not going to let England have their ball back
What is the referee going to do?
Markey's coming back looking very dejected
And he seems to be waiting . . .
He's going back,
Markey is going back for the ball!
What a brilliant and exciting move!
He waited until the front door was closed
And then went back for that ball.
And wait a minute,
He's found it, Markey has found that ball,
He has found the ball
And it's wonderful news
For the hundred thousand fans gathered here
Who are showing their appreciation
In no uncertain fashion.
But wait a minute,
The door is opening once more.
It's her, it's Mrs Spence
And she's waving her fist
And shouting something I can't quite understand
But I don't think it's encouragement.
And Markey's off,
He's jinked past her on the outside
Dodging this way and that
With Mrs Spence in hot pursuit
And he's past her, he's through,
What skills this boy has!
But Mr Spence is there too,
Mr Spence in the sweeper role
With Rover their dog.

Markey's going to have to pull out all the stops now.
He's running straight at him,
And now he's down, he's down on all fours!
What is he doing?
And Oh my goodness that was brilliant,
That was absolutely brilliant,
He's dived through Spence's legs;
But he's got him,
This rugged stopper has him by the coat
And Rover's barking in there too;
He'll never get out of this one.
But this is unbelievable!
He's got away
He has got away:
He wriggled out of his coat
And left part of his trousers with Rover.
This boy is real dynamite.
He's over the wall
He's clear
They'll never catch him now.
He's down the yard and on his way
And I don't think we're going to see
Any more of Markey
Until it's safe to come home.

Gareth Owen

The Race to Get to Sleep

They're on their marks, they're set,
They're off!

Matthew's kicking off his shoes!
Penny's struggling out of her jumper!
He's ripping off his trousers!
She's got one sock off! Now the other's off!
But Matthew's still winning! No, he's not!
It's Penny! Penny's in the lead!
She's down to her knickers!
She's racing out of the room!
She's racing upstairs!
Matthew's right behind her!
There's a fight on the landing!
There's a scramble at the bathroom door!
It's Penny! It's Matthew! It's . . .
Splash! They're both in the bath!
But there's a hitch!
Matthew's got soap in his eye!
Penny's got soap up her nose!
They're stalling! But no, they're both fine!
They're both out of the bath! They're neck and neck!
It's Matthew! It's Penny! It's Matthew!
Now it's Penny again! She's ahead!
She's first on with her pyjamas!
Now Matthew's catching up! There's nothing in it!
They're climbing into their beds!
Matthew's in the lead with one eye closed!
Now it's Penny again. She's got both closed!
So's Matthew! He's catching up!

It's impossible to tell who's winning!
They're both absolutely quiet!
There's not a murmur from either of them.
It's Matthew! It's Penny! It's . . .
It's a draw! A draw!
But no! Wait a moment! It's not a draw!
Matthew's opened an eye!
He's asking if Penny's asleep yet!
He's disqualified!
So's Penny! She's doing the same!
She's asking if Matthew's asleep yet!
It's impossible! It's daft!
It's the hardest race in the world!

Brian Patten

Creative Writing

My story on Monday began:
> *Mountainous seas crashed on the cliffs,*
> *And the desolate land grew wetter . . .*
The teacher wrote a little note: *Remember the capital letter!*

My poem on Tuesday began:
> *Red tongues of fire,*
> *Licked higher and higher*
> *From smoking Etna's top...*
The teacher wrote a little note: *Where is your full stop?*

My story on Wednesday began:
> *Through the lonely, pine-scented wood*
> *There twists a hidden path . . .*
The teacher wrote a little note: *Start a paragraph!*

My poem on Thursday began:
> *The trembling child,*
> *Eyes dark and wild,*
> *Frozen midst the fighting . . .*
The teacher wrote a little note: *Take care untidy writing!*

My story on Friday began:
> *The boxer bruised and bloody lay,*
> *His eye half closed and swollen*
The teacher wrote a little note: *Use a semi-colon!*

Next Monday my story will begin:
> *Once upon a time . . .*

Gervase Phinn

Tidying Up

Put the shot putt
In the sports hut, and
Slam the sports hut door shut.
OK –
That's the shot putt
Put in the hut
Shut up safely for the night.
All right,
Stick the javelin in the equipment bin,
The vaulting pole in the hidey hole,
Slide the rackets in their packets,
Hide the cricket stumps and running pumps,
The shuttlecocks and smellysocks,
Take the shiny shorts across the courts
And put the vaulting vests inside their chests.
Then store the brightly bouncing batting balls
Inside the sports hall.
Er . . . that's all.

Simon Pitt

I'm Not Scared of Ghosts

I'm not, really, I'm not.
It's the things that they drop
with a very loud thump
that give me a shock
and make me jump.
But I'm not scared of ghosts –

No, I'm n . . . o . . . t!

Janis Priestley

I Didn't Want to Come to Your Party Anyway

May your jelly never wobble
May your custard turn to lumps
May your toffee go all gooey
And your mousse come out in bumps

May your pancakes hit the ceiling
May your cocoa crack the cup
May your lollies turn to water
And your sponge cake soak it up

May the icing on your birthday cake
Set hard as superglue
And they'll tell me, "Wish we hadn't
Been invited – just like you!"

Rita Ray

Leisure Centre, Pleasure Centre

Through plate glass doors
    with giant red handles,
into light that's as bright
    as a million candles,
chlorine smells, the whole place steaming
    kids are yelling, kids are screaming.

Watch them
        wave jump
        dive thump
        cartwheel
        free wheel
        look cute
        slip chute
        toe stub
        nose rub
in the leisure centre, pleasure centre.

Sporty people laugh and giggle
    folk in swimsuits give a wiggle,
kids in the café are busy thinkin'
    if they can afford some fizzy drinkin'.
In the changing rooms the wet folk shiver,
    it's hard to get dressed as you shake and quiver.

And we go
        breast stroke
        back stroke
        two-stroke
        big folk

hair soak
little folk
eye poke
no joke
in the leisure centre, pleasure centre.

And now we're driving back home,
fish 'n' chips in the car,
eyes are slowly closing
but it's not very far.
Snuggle-wuggle up in fresh clean sheets
a leisure centre trip is the best of treats!

Because you can
keep fit
leap sit
eat crisps
do twists
belly flop
pit stop
fill up
with 7-Up
get going
blood flowing
look snappy
be happy
in the leisure centre, pleasure centre.

John Rice

September Shoe Rap

De only good ting
bout back to school
is buying new shoes
and playing de fool.

September here,
summer garn,
mi trainers off
mi new shoes on!

Mi mum say Gial
ya playin no more
keep bright, black shoe
from nine till four.

From nine till four
I sit in school,
but on mi way home
I forget de rules.

I run in de grass
kick up de dust
mi bright, black shoe
their shine don't last.

Mi mum see mi shoe,
she look real mean.
She get out the cloth
and make me clean.

I polish mi shoe
and they shine bright.
Me new, black shoes
make September all right.

Chris Riley

The Torch

I nagged my mum and dad for a torch.
"Oh go on. I'd love a torch.
One of those ones with black rubber round them.
Go on. Pleeeeeeese."
It was no good. I wasn't getting anywhere.

Then came my birthday.
On the table was a big box
in the box
a torch.
My dad took it out the box.
"You see that torch," he says
"It's waterproof.
That is a waterproof torch."

Waterproof. Wow!

So that night I got into the bath
and went underwater swimming with it.
Breathe in,
under the water,
switch on
search for shipwrecks
and treasure.
Up, breathe
under again
exploring the ocean floor.

Then the torch went out.

I shook it and banged it but it wouldn't go.
I couldn't get it to go again.
My birthday torch.

So I got out, dried myself off
put on my pyjamas and went into the kitchen.

"The – er – torch won't work. It's broken."
And my dad says,
"What do you mean, 'it's broken'?
It couldn't have just broken.
How did it break?"
"I dunno, it just went off."

"I don't believe it. You ask him a simple question
and you never get a simple answer.
You must have been
doing something with it."
"No. It just went off."
"Just try telling the truth, will you?
How
did
it break?"
"I was underwater swimming with it."

"Are you mad?
When I said the torch is waterproof
I meant it keeps the rain off.
I didn't mean you could go deep-sea diving with it.
Ruined. Completely ruined.
For weeks and weeks he nags us stupid that he wants
one of these waterproof torches
and then first thing he does is wreck it.
How long did it last?
Two minutes? Three minutes?
These things cost money, you know.
Money."

I felt so rotten.
My birthday torch.

At the weekend, he says,
"We're going to Harrow to take the torch back."

We walk into the shop,
my dad goes up to the man at the counter
and says:
"You see this torch.
I bought it from you a couple of weeks ago.
It's broken."

So the man picks it up.
"It couldn't have just broken," says the man,
"how did it break?"
And my dad says,
"I dunno, it just went off."
"Surely you must have been doing something
with it."
"No, no, no," says my dad,
"it just went off."
"Come on," says the man, "these torches don't just break
down."
So I said
"Well, actually, I was in the – "
and I got a hard kick on the ankle from my dad.
"I was in the, you know, er kitchen and it went off."

So the man said that he would take it out the back
to show Len.
He came back a few minutes later and said that Len
couldn't get it to work either
so he would send it back to the makers.
"You'll have to have a new one," he says.
"I should think so too," says my dad.

"Thank YOU."

Outside the shop
my dad says to me,
"What the matter with you?
Are you crazy!
You were going to tell him all about your underwater
swimming fandango, weren't you?
Blabbermouth!"

Michael Rosen

Lost Property
(the Headteacher's announcement)

"Hmm, hmm . . .

A sandwich has been spotted
In the corner of the hall,
Some say it has the odour
To anaesthetize us all;
It has crawled behind the benches,
Adding fluff balls to its grime,
And rolled under the wall-bars –
Must have been there for some time.

Miss Pope says, though she's not certain,
That she's seen it twice before;
Once sliding in the gym, then squashed
Underneath the library door.
And about a month ago, I've heard,
Mr Scott, our new caretaker,
Complained of mouldy, doughy smells
From behind a radiator.

If this over-active, aged lunch,
Well-past its sell-by date,
Belongs to you then please act now
Before it is too late.
Lost property just cannot cope
With items that are squidgy,
Might I suggest unwanted food
Be returned home to your fridgy.

Hmm, hmm . . . Thank you."

Coral Rumble

94

The Bungalowner

I am a bungalowner,
I own a bungalow.
You'd never find a better home
No matter where you go.

We Bungalowners never
Put on fancy airs,
And even if we drink too much
We don't fall down the stairs.

Everyone is equal,
That's what we always say.
We don't look down on anyone;
How could we anyway?

We've only got one storey;
For me just one will do.
I'll never rise to dizzy heights,
And never wanted to.

Come on you bungalowners!
Leave crowsnests to the crows;
So all together everyone:
I OWN A BUNGALOW!

Vernon Scannell

What the headteacher said when he saw me running out of school at 1.15 pm on 21 July last year to buy an ice cream from Pellozzi's van

Hey!*

Fred Sedgwick

* This poem is an attempt on three world records at once: the longest title, the longest footnote, and the shortest text of any poem in the western world. It has been lodged with *The Guinness Book of Records*.

Eighteen Flavours

Eighteen luscious, scrumptious flavours –
Chocolate, lime and cherry,
Coffee, pumpkin, fudge-banana,
Caramel cream and boysenberry,
Rocky road and toasted almond,
Butterscotch, vanilla dip,
Butter-brickle, apple ripple,
Coconut and mocha chip,
Brandy peach and lemon custard,
Each scoop lovely, smooth, and round,
Tallest ice cream cone in town,
Lying there (sniff) on the ground.

Shel Silverstein

A Chewy Toffee Poem

UH GLUG GLEWING GLOGGEE
GLEET IG ALL THE GLINE

GUNGDAY
GLUESDAY
GENSDAY
GLURSDAY
GLIDAY
GLATTERDAY
GLUNSDAY

GLEWING GLOGGEE'S GLUGGLY

GLORNING
GLOON
ANG GLIGHT

EGGLEGGLY GLEAGLE GLOGGEE
WIG GLAKES YR GLEEGALL GLACK

Matt Simpson

Airmail to a Dictionary

Black is the mellow night
Without the black there would be no white.

Black is the pupil of the eye
Putting colour in the sea's skin and earthen sky.

Black is the oil of the engine
On which this whole world is depending.

Black is light years of space
Holding on its little finger this human race.

Black is the colour of ink
That makes the History books we print.

Black is the army. Wars in the night
Putting on the black to hide the white.

Black is the colour of coal
Giving work to the miners and warmth to the cold.

Black is the strip upon my cardcash
That lets me get money from the Halifax.

Black is the shade of the tree
Sharp in definition against inequality.

Black is the eclipse of the sun
Displaying its power to everyone.

Black is the ink from a history
That shall redefine the dictionary.

Black on black is black is black is
Strong as asphalt and tarmac is.

Black is a word that I love to see
Black is that, yeah, black is me.

Lemn Sissay

Kisses!

Last week
my face was smothered in kisses
Yes – **KISSES!**

First there was the **dribbly-wibbly kiss**
when Mum slurped all over me
like an eight mouthed octopus. ("There's my favourite
    boy!")
Then there was the **lipstick-redstick kiss**
when my aunty's rosy lips
painted themselves on my cheeks ("Isn't he so handsome!")
Next came the **flutter-eye, butterfly kiss**
when my girlfriend smoochy-cooched
and fluttered her eyelashes at the same time.
    ("OOOOOOOH!")
After that there was the **soggy-doggy kiss**
when our pet Labrador Sally
tried to lick my face off. ("Slop! Slop! Woof!")
Following that there was **"watch out here I come" miss-kiss**
when my little sister aimed for me
but missed and kissed the cat instead.
    ("UUUUUUUUURGH!")
Then there was the **spectacular-Dracula kiss**
when my cousin Isabel leapt from behind the shower
    curtain
and attacked my neck. ("AAAAAAAAAAGH – suck!")
Of course, there was the **"sssssssssh don't tell anyone"**
    self-kiss
when I looked in the bathroom mirror
and kissed myself. (Once was enough!)

But the unbeatable, second to none, zing-dinger of a kiss
came from Gran.
It was a lipsucking, cheek plucking, Donald Ducking,
SMACKEROONY OF A KISS. (She'd forgotten to put
   her teeth in!)

Ian Souter

Louder!

OK, Andrew, nice and clearly – off you go.

Welcome everybody to our school concert . . .

Louder, please, Andrew. Mums and dads won't hear you at the back, will they?

Welcome everybody to our school concert . . .

Louder, Andrew. You're not trying.
Pro – ject – your – voice.
Take a b i g b r e a t h and louder!

Welcome everybody to our school concert . . .

For goodness sake, Andrew. LOUDER! LOUDER!

Welcome every body to our school concert!

Now, Andrew, there's no need to be silly.

Roger Stevens

Smile

Smile, go on, smile!
Anyone would think, to look at you,
that your cat was on the barbecue
or your best friend had died.
Go on, curve your mouth.
Take a look at that beggar,
or that one-legged bus conductor.
Where's *your* cross?
Smile, slap your thigh.
Hiccup, make a horse noise,
lollop through the house,
fizz up your coffee.
Take down your guitar
from its air-shelf and play
imaginary reggae
out through the open door.
And smile, remember, smile,
give those teeth some sun,
grin at everyone,
do it now, go on, SMILE!

Matthew Sweeney

The Gruesome Gambols of Gertrude Ghoul

Grim, grisly Gertrude, a gruesome green ghoul,
grew bored with her graveyard and grouched off to school.
Going in, growling, she pushed her way past
Miss Grimble, a teacher, who gasped, quite aghast.
"Great costume," a girl said, "all grotty and green,
but has anyone mentioned it's not Hallowe'en."
"I'm grumpy," growled Gertrude, "I'm gory and grim
but you, gawping gaby, are gormless and dim."
Then she grabbed at the girl with a giggle of glee.
"Good grief!" groaned Miss Grimble, "just set that girl
          free.
We've a ghoul here already as gruesome as you.
Glum Gilbert's so gloomy, we couldn't stand two."
"I'll get him," Gert grated, "and grind him to sludge.
Just call me," she grumbled, "a ghoul with a grudge."
A door was groped open. A ghoul gloomed in sight.
Glum Gilbert stood goggling, in love at first fright.
"Good gad," gloated Gilbert, "a ghoul, and a girl,
Grotesque, green and gangling, a positive pearl."
He grabbed as she grappled. They gambolled, gyrated.
The kids and Miss Grimble all gawked with breath bated
as gurgling, galumphing, they galloped away.
"Quite gone," grinned Miss Grimble, "at least, for today."

Marian Swinger

Superstar

I WANNA BE A SUPERSTAR.
I wanna drive a massive car.
I wanna join the famous set.
I wanna own a private jet.
I wanna lotta fun at nights.
I wanna name that's up in lights.
I wanna lotta caviar.
I WANNA BE A SUPERSTAR.
I wanna have a lotta fun.
I wanna song at number one.
I wanna be like you-know-who.
I wanna be on TV too.
I wannapplause from near and far.
I WANNA BE A SUPERSTAR.
I wanna wear a lamé suit.
I wanna be a hunky brute.
I wanna have a lotta fun.
I wanna headline in The Sun.
I wanna fill the Palladium.
I wanna fill Wembley Stadium.
I wanna thrash a flash guitar.
I WANNA BE A SUPERSTAR!!!

Charles Thomson

Crusher

I'm a
huge hy-
draulic
crusher.
Read my
base I'm
made in
Russia.
Oiled out
of a
Texas
gusher.
Piston
puller.
Piston
pusher.
Function
like a
toilet
flusher.
I'm a
huge hy-
draulic
crusher.
Made to
be a
metal
musher.

My sur-
roundings
could be
plusher.
Scrap-yard
mud that
should be
lusher.
I work
slowly
I'm no
rusher.
I'm a
huge hy-
draulic
crusher.

Nick Toczek

After the Match

Did yer see the other team!
Thee all 'ad one leg.
'ands tied behind their backs.
Ah've seen better schoolboys round our way
Kicking ball in't street.
Their kits were rubbish.
Thee didn't even look the part,
More like rag and bone men.
Feller who trained 'em should ha'
Taught 'em to play football
Not nancy around with the ball
Like ballet dancers.
An' another thing
That ref was blind
Or thee'd never ha' won.

Angela Topping

Line-Up

It's Tim's team
versus Saeed's side.
At kick-off
Col and I collide.
Cheryl's cheering.
Rita meets
Sharon's challenge.
Pete competes.
Rashid rushes
Ali's attack.
Clare's clearance
hits Barry's back.
Mark's marking
Chris's sister.
Liam limps off
with a blister.
Louise loses.
Ted will head.
The ball balloons out.
Ted goes red.
Linus is linesman.
He says throw in.
Carrie's hacked down
in a clash with Glyn.
Tracey's the trainer;
and Ralph the Ref
hears her shout out –
or is he deaf?
He stops the game,
and has a quick cough

as the casualty, Carrie,
is carried off.

As play restarts,
it's as before.
Karen runs,
but will she score?
Rod nods down
and jinks past Jill.
A quick flick on
and it's one-nil.

Jill Townsend

Batman

Batman
Age 10½
Patrols the streets of his suburb
At night
Between 7 and 8 o'clock.
If he is out later than this
he is spanked
and sent to bed
Without supper.

Batman
Almost 11
Patrols the streets of his suburb
At night
If he has finished his homework.

Batman,
His secret identity
And freckles
Protected
By the mask and cloak
His Auntie Elsie
Made on her sewing machine,
Patrols
At night
Righting Wrongs.

Tonight he is on the trail of
Raymond age 11
(large for his age)
Who has stolen Stephen's
Gobstoppers and football cards.

Batman
Patrolling the streets of his suburb
Righting Wrongs
Finds Raymond,
Demands the return of the stolen goods.
Raymond knocks him over,
Rips his mask,
Tears his cloak,
And steals his utility belt.
Batman starts to cry,
Wipes his eyes with his cape
(His hankie was in the belt).

Next day
Auntie Elsie says
This is the fourteenth time
I've had to mend your
Batman costume.
If it happens again
You'll have to whistle for it.

Batman
Eats a bag of crisps.

John Turner

Hard to Please

I don't like stings from wasps or bees
I don't like friends to see my knees
I don't like war, don't like disease
That's why they call me hard to please.

I don't like milk that smells like cheese
I don't like coughs that start to wheeze
I don't like spots you have to squeeze
That's why they call me hard to please.

I don't like baths that start to freeze
I don't like friends who taunt and tease
I don't like last week's mushy peas
That's why they call me hard to please.

Steve Turner

Studup

"Owaryer?"
"Imokay."
"Gladtwearit."
"Howbowchew?"
"Reelygrate."
"Binwaytinlong?"
"Longinuff."
"Owlongubinear?"
"Boutanour."
"Thinkeelturnup?"
"Aventaclue."
"Dewfancyim?"
"Sortalykim."
"Wantadrinkorsummat?"
"Thanksilestayabit."
"Soocherself."
"Seeyalater."
"Byfernow."

Barrie Wade

there were these two girls

there were these two girls
strutting down the street
whistling
loud enough to crack the windows

they were whistling
at the moon
but the moon just winked
as it hid behind a cloud

they were whistling
at the lamp-posts
but the lamp-posts just blinked
as they leaned together
like drunks

they were whistling
at the boys
who slinked off round the corner
like shamefaced puppies
with their tails between their legs

they were whistling
at the world
then they stood there listening
to see
if the world would whistle back

Dave Ward

Blood and Bones

Under the floorboards, cold and deep,
Pipes are laid that drip and seep.
Down below the house, in the damp, dark mud,
Do they drip water or do they drip . . . ?

> *Blood in my arteries!*
> *Blood in my veins!*
> *I dreamt that blood ran*
>   *down the drains!*

High above the ceilings rafters creak.
Blind bats blunder. Mad mice squeak.
Up in the roof there are rattles and moans.
Is it the wind or chains and . . . ?

> *Bones in my body!*
> *Bones in my head!*
> *I dreamt there was a skeleton*
>   *in my bed!*

Celia Warren

Oogles and Splodges

Oogles and Splodges
And Ninkles and Nodges
All make me go rigid with fright.
'Coz they flash through my dreams
Never ending it seems
As I lie in my bed every night.

There's Mombles and Chillies
And Dongles and Zillies,
And Haggles and Boggles and Yeets.
And all I can do
Is cry softly "Boo-hoo"
As I quickly dive under the sheets.

But then comes the dawn,
And the creatures have gone,
The nightmares have finished it seems.
But come ten o'clock
They'll all run amok
And chase me again through my dreams.

Clive Webster

Vitamin Pills

Vitamin pills, vitamin pills,
Give me A, B, C, D, E.
Yes, it's vitamin pills forever,
And a healthy life for me.

I take Vitamin A
At breakfast
With my sugar
Coated flakes.

I take Vitamin B
At elevenses
With my cream and
Chocolate cakes.

I take Vitamin C
At dinner
With my sausages
And chips.

I take Vitamin D
At break time
With my crisps
And walnut whips.

I take vitamin E
At supper
With my burger,
So you see,

It's vitamin pills forever
And a healthy life for me!

Colin West

Is Your Mum Like This?

My mum
wears
Deely-boppers
Silver-spangled tights
Tank tops
CND earrings
Bunches
An eye-patch
Fifteen bangles
 (on each arm)
Leg-warmers
Platforms
Ra-ra skirts and flares
(together at the same time)
A monocle
Pom-poms
Headphones
Fingerless gloves
A top hat
and tails
And that's just
To go shopping.

Jane Wright

Watch Out, Walter Wall!

The king of carpet salesmen
Is a man called Walter Wall.
He's got a shop next door to us
He used to think too small.
And so he asked permission, please,
To alter WALTER WALL.

"What? Alter WALTER WALL?" the Council
Cried. "Why? What's the call?"
"My rugs are filling up with bugs
From standing in the hall.
My place has got no stacking-space –
No space," said Walt, "at all!"

The Council said, "Go right ahead.
Don't falter, Walter Wall!
It's alteration stations, Walter.
Sideways, build a tall
Extension, that will form an extra
Wall to WALTER WALL!"

And so across the taller wall
I call to Walter Wall
And over it I often boot
A ball to Walter Wall.
Likewise the cat can crawl the wall
And *fall* to Walter Wall!

So everything has worked out well:
More space for Walter Wall.
The cat and I have got a place
To crawl, fall, boot a ball:

And often, I am proud to say,
The cat and ball, instead
Of landing on the carpets, clout
Old Walt *hard* on the head!

Kit Wright

Body Talk

Dere's a Sonnet
Under me bonnet
Dere's an Epic
In me ear,
Dere's a Novel
In me navel
Dere's a classic
Here somewhere.
Dere's a Movie
In me left knee
A long story
In me right,
Dere's a shorty
Inbetweeny
It is tickly
In de night.
Dere's a picture
In me ticker
Unmixed riddims
In me heart,
In me texture
Dere's a comma
In me fat chin
Dere is Art.
Dere's an Opera
In me bladder
A Ballad's
In me wrist
Dere is laughter
In me shoulder

In me guzzard's
A nice twist.
In me dreadlocks
Dere is syntax
A dance kicks
In me bum
Thru me blood tacks
Dere run true facts
I got limericks
From me Mum,
Documentaries
In me entries
Plays on history
In me folk,
Dere's a Trilogy
When I tink of three
On me toey
Dere's a joke.

Benjamin Zephaniah

Bath-Time

bath-time wasn't easy
with seventeen of us
and the dog
plus we'd throw the goldfish in
to give him a good swim

we were deprived of bubbles
suds and bath oils
no avocado and chocolate mousse shampoo for us
no namby pamby eau de toilette
Mam used to throw in a bit of bleach
to make us come out rosy

rubber ducks were considered a luxury
so we floated the frozen chicken
for tomorrow's Sunday dinner
and torpedoed it with loofers

getting dry was difficult with only one tea-towel
no fire
and a hole in the roof

we'd sit around a candle and tell stories
while the hole let in the starlight
and the soot from next door's chimney
that covered us from head to foot
in black, burnt dirt

"Just look at the state of you," Mam would say
"You need a good bath"

Ann Ziety

Copyright Acknowledgements

The Compiler and publishers would like to thank the following for permission to reprint the selections in this book.

John Agard and Caroline Sheldon Literary Agency for 'Spell to Banish a Pimple', first published in *Life Doesn't Scare Me At All* by Heinemann.

Jez Alborough for 'A Smile'.

SuAndi for 'Everybody Rap'.

Moira Andrew for 'My Gran'.

Leo Aylen for 'Micky Hackett's Rocket', first published in *Rhymoceros* by Macmillan.

Gerard Benson for 'A Tale of Two Citizens'.

Valerie Bloom for 'Haircut Rap'.

Margaret Blount for 'Tidyholic'.

Stephen Bowkett for 'The Shapeshifter's Riddle'.

Sandy Brownjohn for 'Catnap in the Catnip'.

Dave Calder for 'Assembly', first published in *Creepy Poems* by Usborne.

Charles Causley and David Higham Associates for 'Out in the Desert' from *Collected Poems* published by Macmillan Children's Books.

Debjani Chatterjee for 'My Sari'.

John Coldwell for 'Wrestling with Mum'.

Andrew Collett for 'What is an Alien?'.

Paul Cookson for 'Sea Shoals See Shows on the Sea Bed'.

John Cooper Clarke for 'Haiku'.

Wendy Cope for 'An Attempt at Unrhymed Verse'.

Pie Corbett for 'The Playground Monster', first published in *Another First Poetry Book* by Oxford University Press.

John Cotton for 'Class Three's Affections'.

Sue Cowling for 'Well, You Shouldn't Have . . . '.

John Cunliffe for 'Standing Up to Read a Poem In Front of All These People'.

Jan Dean for 'Ghosts In Our Suburban Homes'.

John C. Desmond for 'Team Talk'.

Peter Dixon for 'Meryl Rose'.

Gina Douthwaite for 'Night Mer'.

Carol Ann Duffy for 'Chocs'.

Richard Edwards for 'Some Favourite Words'.

John Foster for 'Shaun Short's Short Shorts'.

Pam Gidney for 'A Perfect Match'.

Martin Glynn for 'Wurd Up'.

Mick Gowar for 'Boots'.

Philip Gross for 'Daughter of the Sea', first published in *The All-Nite Café* by Faber and Faber.

Mike Harding for 'Semantricks'.

David Harmer for 'Mister Moore'.

Trevor Harvey for 'The Painting Lesson', first published in *Funny Poems* by Usborne.

John Hegley for 'On the Pavement', first published in *Love Cuts* by Methuen.

Stewart Henderson for 'Tiger'.

Adrian Henri for 'Best Friends', first published in *The Phantom Lollipop Lady* by Methuen. Reproduced by permission of the the author c/o Rogers, Coleridge and White Ltd.

David Horner for 'Just Fancy That . . .'.

Libby Houston for 'Shop Chat'.

Ted Hughes for 'My Granny', first published in *Meet My Folks* by Faber and Faber.

Elizabeth Jennings and David Higham Associates for 'My Shops'.

Mike Johnson for 'Iced Ink'.

Jenny Joseph for 'Going Out With Mum.'

Mike Jubb for 'Rockets'.

Jackie Kay for 'Hairpin Bend', first published in *Two's Company* by Puffin.

Jean Kenward for 'The Newcomer'.

Tony Langham for 'Nothing Tastes Quite Like a Gerbil'.

Roger McGough for 'A Gottle of Geer', first published in *Bad Bad Cats* by Viking. Reprinted by permission of the Peters Fraser and Dunlop Group Ltd.

Ian McMillan and Martyn Wiley for 'Biggles Flies To Barnsley'.

Colin McNaughton and Walker Books for 'Teef, Teef', first published in *There's An Awful Lot of Weirdos in Our Neighbourhood* by Walker Books Limited.

Lindsay MacRae for '2 Poems About 4 Eyes' first published in *You Canny Shove Yer Granny off a Bus* by Puffin Books.

Wes Magee for 'In the Misty, Murky Graveyard'.

Gerda Mayer for 'The Crunch', first published in *The Candy-Floss Tree* by Oxford University Press.

Trevor Millum for 'The Dark Avenger', first published in *Double Talk* by Stove Creek Press.

Adrian Mitchell for 'Dumb Insolence', published in *Adrian Mitchell's Greatest Hits* by Bloodaxe Books. Reprinted by permission of the Peters Fraser and Dunlop Group Ltd. Educational Health Warning! Adrian Mitchell asks that none of his poems are used in connection with any examinations whatsoever.

Tony Mitton and David Higham Associates for 'Forbidden Poem'.

Michaela Morgan for 'Food for Thought'.

Brian Moses for 'Peasy!', first published in *The Usborne Book of Children's Poems* by Usborne.

Judith Nicholls for 'Caliban's Cave'.

Henry Normal for 'Love Conquers All (A Love Poem for Dyslexics)'.

David Orme for 'Bigfoot'.

Jack Ousbey for 'Gran Can You Rap?'.

Gareth Owen for 'The Commentator', first published in *Song of the City* by HarperCollins. Reproduced by permission of the author c/o Rogers, Coleridge and White Ltd.

Brian Patten for 'The Race to Get to Sleep', first published in *Thawing*

Frozen Frogs by Puffin Books.

Gervase Phinn for 'Creative Writing'.

Simon Pitt for 'Tidying Up', first published in *Does W Trouble U?* by Viking Books.

Janis Priestley for 'I'm Not Scared of Ghosts'.

Rita Ray for 'I Didn't Want to Come to Your Party Anyway', first published in *Food* by Wayland Publishers.

John Rice for 'Leisure Centre, Pleasure Centre'.

Chris Riley for 'September Shoe Rap'.

Michael Rosen for 'The Torch' first published in 'You Wait Till I'm Older Than You' by Viking.

Coral Rumble for 'Lost Property'.

Vernon Scannell for 'The Bungalowner'.

Fred Sedgwick for 'What the Headteacher Said', first published in *Two by Two* by Tricky Sam! Press.

Shel Silverstein for 'Eighteen Flavours' from *Where the Sidewalk Ends* by HarperCollins. Reprinted by permission of Edite Kroll Literary Agency Inc.

Matt Simpson for 'A Chewy Toffee Poem'.

Lemn Sissay for 'Airmail to a Dictionary'.

Ian Souter for 'Kisses'.

Roger Stevens for 'Louder'.

Matthew Sweeney for 'Smile', first published in *Fatso in the Red Suit* by Faber and Faber.

Marian Swinger for 'The Gruesome Gambols of Gertrude Ghoul'.

Charles Thompson for 'Superstar'.

Nick Toczek for 'Crusher'.

Angela Topping for 'After the Match'.

Jill Townsend for 'Line-Up'.

John Turner for 'Batman', first published in *Hard Shoulders, Second Home* by Versewagon Press.

Steve Turner for 'Hard to Please', first published in *The Day I Fell Down The Toilet* by Lion Publishing plc.

Barrie Wade for 'Studup'.

Dave Ward for 'there were these two girls', first published in *Candy and Jazz* by Oxford University Press.

Celia Warren for 'Blood and Bones'.

Clive Webster for 'Oogles and Splodges'.

Colin West for 'Vitamin Pills'.

Jane Wright for 'Is Your Mum Like This?'.

Kit Wright for 'Watch Out, Walter Wall!'.

Benjamin Zephaniah for 'Body Talk'.

Anne Ziety for 'Bath-Time'.

All possible care has been taken to trace the ownership of every selection included and to make full acknowledgement for its use. If any errors have accidentally occured, they will be corrected in subsequent editions, provided notification is sent to the publishers.